Wheels around Fort William and Lo

by
Robert Grieves

Corran Ferry, plying across the narrows of Loch Linnhe from Nether Lochaber to Ardgour, did not become motorised until the mid-1930s when the ferry rights were transferred from Inverness and Argyll County Councils to Mr Mackintosh of Nether Lochaber Hotel. Its inception as a vehicular ferry at that time was long overdue, avoiding a 45 mile detour by road via Fort William and Kinlocheil. This scene from that period shows an Austin 16 on board, with the whitewashed Ardgour Hotel visible on the far shore, while a young girl gazes on wistfully. The Austin's cabriolet bodywork by Tickford incorporated a fold-down canvas roof which was fully open on this occasion, indicating a mild summer day.

The publishers regret that they cannot supply copies of any pictures featured in this book.

ACKNOWLEDGEMENTS

A. W. Brotchie, Aberdour; Donald Cameron, St Catherine's; Dan MacDonald, Roy Bridge; Miss D. M. MacIntyre, Fort William; Ian Maclean, Bishopton; Andy Paton, Caol; John Sinclair, Milngavie; W. A. C. Smith, Glasgow; R. J. S. Wiseman, Richmond; Ballachulish Hotel; The Omnibus Society.

The south-eastern edge of Lochaber fringes the bleak Rannoch Moor. This view from around 1930 looking across a couple of lochans towards Blackcorries shows a Vauxhall saloon of the period driving south on the unmade gravel road between Glencoe and Tyndrum. The present highway lies several hundred yards across the moor. It was not until 1934 that the new A82 Glasgow to Fort William road was completed and in several places it follows a different alignment to the original route. For instance from Bridge of Orchy the old road rounded the western end of Loch Tulla, past Inveroran Hotel and Victoria Bridge then headed almost directly north over the Black Mount, whereas its successor takes the east side of Loch Tulla and continues well to the east of the earlier way until rejoining near Kingshouse Hotel. This section of the old road was described in early twentieth century guidebooks as 'very rough and stony' and 'in heavy rains more like a river bed'. In May 1927 the *Highland News* reported that it was 'almost impossible to drive over the Glencoe road without damage to the motor car and possibly one's limbs as well', and travel writer H. V. Morton declared it 'the worst road in Scotland' in his 1929 publication *In Search of Scotland*. This doubtful honour passed to the Mallaig road when the new Glencoe road was officially opened in 1934. It was hardly surprising, therefore, that MacBraynes waited until its completion before inaugurating their much-heralded through service by motor coach between Glasgow and Fort William in 1934.

2

FOREWORD

For this latest offering in the *Wheels around* series I have chosen Fort William and Lochaber, an area of Scotland which for many years was particularly dependent on the services of David MacBrayne for both public and freight transport, by land and sea (and canal!). This perhaps explains the inclusion of what some might think are a disproportionate number of views of MacBrayne vehicles and vessels. For this I make no apology since the company played such an important part in the transport life of the town and surrounding districts, and accordingly employed many local people. Admittedly I have a personal interest in MacBraynes as I retain happy memories of my days working as a conductor and then driver on their colourful red, green and cream buses in the 1960s.

The Fort William area has long been a magnet for visitors wishing to enjoy its superb surroundings, including our highest mountain, Ben Nevis, of course. Many more were able to travel to the town with the arrival of the railway in 1894 and within a further few years the first motor cars appeared on the scene.

The Caledonian Canal and Glencoe were also main attractions and the early horse coach and later motor charabanc proprietors were not slow to make the most of this potential. But let the photographs tell the story.

'A Hearty Welcome to Fort William' proclaims the banner across the specially built decorated archway spanning the west end of the High Street at the courthouse. The occasion was the visit of King Edward VII to the town and to Mamore Lodge in 1909. The imposing open car in the foreground is ST 96, a Daimler 30/45 h.p. model which according to the Inverness-shire motor tax records had been purchased in September 1906 by Edward Gooch of Torcastle, Banavie, and was painted in a dark chocolate colour. Hopefully Mr Gooch turned around in time to notice and avoid the Scottie uncomfortably close to the car.

Our Victorian relatives enjoyed travel just as much as we do now, although longer journeys tended to be affordable only to those in the higher income brackets. Railway and steamer services helped to popularise areas which had been out of reach both physically and financially to many. One such area was historic Glencoe which attracted many summer visitors who took advantage of the various circular tours organised by the rail, steamer and coach companies which were quick to see the potential tourist traffic. These late 1890s scenes show five-in-hand coaches with well-dressed tourist passengers enjoying the grandeur of Glencoe. Connections were made at Ballachulish pier with MacBraynes steamer *Fusilier* which sailed from Oban to Fort William at 6 a.m. and 12.30 p.m. and with the *Mountaineer* at 9.15 a.m.

Mountaineer passengers also had the choice of joining the Glencoe and Glenetive coach which in turn connected with the sailing of SS *Ossian* on Loch Etive from Lochetivehead to Achnacloich where the train was joined to complete the circle back to Oban. Alternatively, the *Mountaineer* sailing additionally connected at Ballachulish with Cameron's horse-drawn coach which continued through Glencoe via Clachaig Inn to Kingshouse Inn then over the Black Mount to Inveroran Hotel and Bridge of Orchy station where the midday train to Glasgow was met. All these places were on the old highway before the route altered with the construction of the new road in the early 1930s. Dougie Cameron's horses and coaches were based at his Inveroran Hotel, but were additionally changed at Kingshouse Hotel in each direction to and from Ballachulish which was most necessary after their long climb over Black Mount or Glencoe. The last of these horse coaches continued to operate into the 1920s by which time motorised opposition had appeared in the form of charabancs. This view shows the coach pausing at Loch Triochtan allowing the photographer to capture Glencoe's loch and mountain scenery.

Scotland's west coast ferries have always been important short cuts along our Atlantic seaboard, where the deeply indented coastline involves lengthy detours to negotiate around the sea lochs by road. Historically most of these ferries have been operated for several centuries and some still have their traditional ferry inns on each side of the crossing. One of the best-known was Ballachulish Ferry which sailed across the narrows where Loch Leven meets Loch Linnhe and avoided considerable extra drive time via Kinlochleven. It was replaced by a bridge in 1975, relieving the frustrating traffic queues which built up on both sides of the crossing, especially during each summer season. Taken in 1911, this view shows a car being rowed across with Ballachulish Hotel just visible on the misty shore.

Even in the earlier years of the motor ferries cars suffered long delays since initially just one vehicle could be carried. When the road around Loch Leven was reconstructed and greatly improved in the early 1930s many motorists opted to avoid the ferry delays, preferring to drive the sixteen extra miles via Kinlochleven. Both this picture and the one above show the precarious manner in which vehicles were transported in the early days as it was not until 1912 that a motor ferry replaced the old rowing boat on which Edwardian automobiles were required to balance primitively on planks. This vehicle, a Daimler registered DU 5518, was one of the last cars to cross on the old ferry in 1912. It is seen here about to disembark down the planks at North Ballachulish.

The replacement motorised craft for Ballachulish Ferry arrived in July 1912 and was obviously a great improvement over the previous rowing boat, giving motorists a degree of peace of mind which they could not possibly have enjoyed when balanced precariously on planks. The boat, named *Glencoe*, was built on the Gareloch by McGruer & Co. of Clynder to the design and order of the Robertson Engineering Co. Ltd. of North Street, Glasgow, agents for the tenants of the ferry. It was fitted with a 15–20 h.p. Kelvin engine. To test the capabilities of *Glencoe*, a Paisley-built Arrol–Johnston lorry (XS 184) which belonged to Robertson's was loaded on the turntable with several brave gentlemen to conduct stability trials and was therefore the first vehicle to drive aboard. The ticket illustrated was issued on one of the last Ballachulish Ferry crossings in 1975.

The Ballachulish Ferry arrives with a puff of exhaust smoke at the North Ballachulish landing in 1931 with a big Austin 16 saloon. A group of hikers prepares to board, possibly from the nearby Alltshellach House, home to the Holiday Fellowship. Interestingly, around this time there was a proposed scheme to build a transporter-type bridge (as at Middlesbrough on Teesside) at this location across the narrows but of course this did not materialise, and it took a further 45 years before Ballachulish Bridge eventually opened, the final ferry sailing on 23 December 1975. The motor ferry seen here was successor to the original motor boat *Glencoe* which had plied the narrows of Loch Leven since replacing the old rowing boat in July 1912.

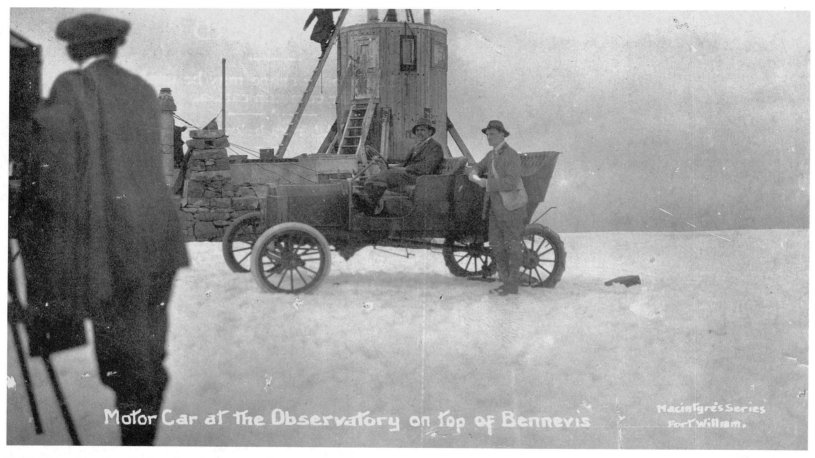

Motor Car at the Observatory on top of Bennevis

Macintyre's Series
Fort William.

Fort William boasts on its doorstep the commanding presence of 4,412 foot Ben Nevis, our highest mountain. Accordingly it was a great attraction for status-seeking individuals and companies advertising their wares. For example, when the motor car was still a relatively newfangled machine within the financial reach of only the more prosperous members of society, an amazing feat in a Ford was accomplished by conquering the Ben. The three-day ascent in a 20 h.p. Model T was successfully completed on 15 May 1911 by Henry Alexander (whose father owned Edinburgh's main Ford agency) in a blaze of glory, particularly for the Ford Motor Co. and Dunlop tyres. The car (S 1871) was left on the summit for the night and descended next day in only two and a half hours, followed by a celebration procession through the town. In addition to the obligatory pipe band and town council reception was Donald MacDougall wheeling a barrow as a reminder that he also had established a record by pushing a wheelbarrow to the summit several years before. Incidentally, A. & J. MacPherson of Gordon Square supplied horses to assist the Ford in its ascent of the Ben, but needless to say this information was not mentioned in the fanfare of publicity which followed.

In 1928 Henry Alexander repeated his feat of seventeen years earlier when he reached the top of Ben Nevis again in a Ford – this time SC 2328 – a new model A, seen here on the ascent. The same year saw another successful car climb of the Ben, when George Simpson arrived at the top in an Austin Seven. Over the years other attempts have been made to climb Ben Nevis by car, including one in 1962 by a group of medical students in an Austin Gypsy and in a Land Rover in 1963, while in 1969 a Gnat reached the top.

A number of motorcycles were also successful, the first of which was an AJS and sidecar ridden by Duncan Bell in 1913. Our picture on the summit shows ST 2952, a 1924 BSA owned by Donald Cameron Sim of Nevis Distillery, surrounded by well-wishers (and their dog). In the background is part of the wall of the former observatory which had been erected by the Scottish Meteorological Society in the 1880s but abandoned in 1904.

On what was the main A82 road (this section became the B863 following the opening of Ballachulish Bridge in the mid-1970s) is an Armstrong–Siddeley tourer of the 1920s, registered MR 5263 in Wiltshire. The photo appears to have been taken shortly after the improved road along the north shore of Loch Leven was opened in 1927, as this section, between Kinlochleven and North Ballachulish looking towards the narrows of Caolsnacoan, seems brand new. Before this it was little better than a rough track. Armstrong–Siddeley cars were built in Coventry until 1960 and their final model was the Star Sapphire.

A similar scene only from high above the previous view, where part of the old military road built by Major Caulfield (successor to General Wade) traverses Mamore between Fort William and Altnafeadh before continuing to Stirling (now partly followed by the West Highland Way). Seen here near Mamore Lodge in the late 1920s is an 18 h.p. Armstrong–Siddeley tourer with the once familiar V-shape radiator and sphinx mascot, carrying London number YN 5794. Its occupants are enjoying the vista across Loch Leven towards the Pap of Glencoe, while behind the car rises the hill known as the Cailleach, or Old Lady.

Younger readers may have wondered how motor vehicles reached the islands before the days of conventional car ferries in the 1960s. The answer is seen here at Mallaig around 1960, when this Vauxhall PA series Cresta was winched aboard MacBraynes outer isles vessel *Lochmor* bound for the Uists and Harris, to join other cars already on deck.

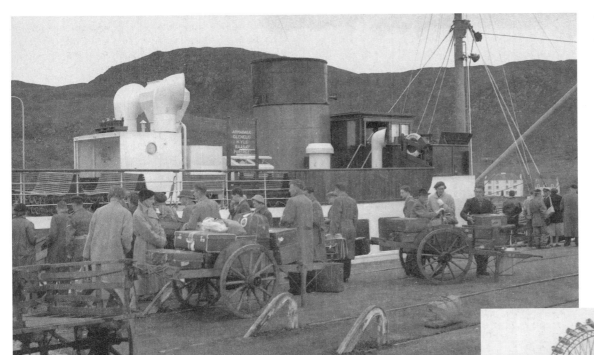

Other wheels in Mallaig around the 1950s and 60s were those of the luggage barrows which carried the suitcases of railway passengers from the station to the pier. This is well-illustrated in this scene showing MV *Lochnevis* loading prior to sailing for Armadale, Glenelg, Kyle, Raasay and Portree, as may be seen from the vessel's destination board.

A wheel with a difference was envisaged for Mallaig by the West Highland Railway Company, whose iron road reached the village in 1901. This contemporary illustration by the artist W. Reynolds appeared in the North British Railway *Beauties of Scotland* official guide in the Edwardian period. It depicts the Mallaig of the future as seen through the eyes of the railway company shareholders who hoped to 'develop' the village as a holiday centre. Fortunately, perhaps, this did not materialise and so Mallaig never became the Blackpool of Scotland and visitors were spared the sight of pierrots on the promenade and a giant Ferris wheel, interesting though the concept may have been.

MALLAIG—TWENTY YEARS HENCE.

On the border of Lochaber and Badenoch is Loch Laggan, popularised lately since becoming better known through the TV series 'Monarch of the Glen', set on the southern shore around Ardverikie House. This mid-1920s scene on the unsealed lochside road looking towards Binnein Shuas on the south side shows the car to be GB 4376, a Buick convertible, one of the many popular American imports of the period. It is heading from Roy Bridge towards Laggan Bridge on what is now the A86, as a lone cyclist passes in the opposite direction.

Lots of lovely lonely roads abound in the Lochaber area and one of my own favourites is the B8043 which leaves the main A884 from Lochaline to head directly for Loch Linnhe. This view shows SS 3100, a Buick of 1930 which had been registered in East Lothian, complete with Union flag and GB plate, suggesting it had travelled outwith Britain. It has paused on the rough road at Camus na Croise, between Kingairloch and Glengalmadale before continuing towards Kilmalieu and Corran along the northern shore of Loch Linnhe.

Spean Bridge station in Edwardian times during the period from 1903 until 1908 when the branch line known as the Invergarry & Fort Augustus Railway was worked by the Highland Railway, whose tank locomotive No. 52 (built in 1893 by Dübs & Co. of Polmadie, Glasgow, and originally intended for the Uruguay Eastern Railway) is seen with an assembly of officials on the platform. When the Highland Railway withdrew from the branch in 1908, the North British Railway stepped in to continue the service but only until 1911 when common sense dictated they could no longer suffer the loss on what was a totally uneconomic line. The I&FA branch thus became one of the earliest examples of Scotland's abandoned railways, setting a trend for what was to become a common occurrence half a century later. The line was advertised for scrap but after much wrangling was reopened two years later with the NBR operating again and continuing until 1933 when passenger traffic was once more withdrawn. Finally on 31 December 1946 the line was closed completely, but even today it is possible to enjoy walking along sections of the former track through the delightful countryside once served by this unfortunate railway.

An artist's impression of Highland Railway 4-4-0 tank loco No. 54 about to enter the short tunnel on the section of track along the side of Loch Oich between Aberchalder and Invergarry. Other wheels may be seen on the waters of the loch in the shape of the paddle steamer *Gondolier* which plied Thomas Telford's Caledonian Canal from Banavie to Inverness. *Gondolier* was a member of the MacBrayne fleet from 1866 until 1939 and served canal and lochside communities in the Great Glen including Gairlochy, Laggan, Cullochy, Fort Augustus, Temple Pier (for Drumnadrochit) and Foyers.

Double-headed steam locomotives climb westwards over 'Concrete Bob' McAlpine's well-known Glenfinnan viaduct with a Mallaig-bound train in the early 1950s pulling the red and cream carriages of this period. Both locos are 2-6-0s, with a 'K1' type leading and a 'K2' acting as pilot. The viaduct has become even better known since appearing in the Harry Potter movie scenes showing Hogwart's Express crossing the 21 famous spans, which have now stood firmly for over a century. 'Concrete Bob' was how Robert McAlpine was familiarly known amongst his civil engineering contemporaries because of his enthusiasm for mass concrete, which was then a relatively untried building medium but was successfully used by him on all the West Highland viaducts. McAlpine was the contractor for the West Highland extension between Fort William and Mallaig, which opened in 1901.

Leaving Fort William station in Edwardian times, North British Railway Co. loco 679 steams along the shore of Loch Linnhe with a train of clerestory-roofed carriages presumably bound for Mallaig on the West Highland extension. 679 was a class 'C' locomotive of 0-6-0 configuration designed by Matthew Holmes and built in 1892 by Sharp, Stewart & Co. of Atlas Works, Springburn, Glasgow. After later rebuilding this particular engine lasted until 1957 with British Railways. Surprisingly, someone decided to defy the specks of soot and cinders from passing trains and has hung washing to dry over the railway fence. Fort William station remained on its lochside site until the arrival of the new shoreside road to relieve the congested High Street. In 1975 the present station opened at the east end of the town.

A Mallaig-bound train departs Banavie station in the mid-1960s, with engine driver and signalman exchanging the 'tablets' which authorise safe entry to the single track section ahead. The swing bridge which carries the railway across the Caledonian Canal may be seen just beyond; this was manually opened and the wheel for this purpose is visible to the left. The original section of the West Highland line from Glasgow to Fort William opened in August 1894 and contractor Robert McAlpine completed the Mallaig extension for opening in April 1901. The route was dieselised in 1962 when the long era of steam ended, and this 'type 2' (later class 27) Sulzer-engined loco, built by the Birmingham Railway Carriage & Wagon Works, was typical of those used. Steam traction may again be enjoyed on the Mallaig line having been reintroduced in 1984 using preserved locomotives, and these summer steam operations now help attract even more visitors to Lochaber.

Below right: The British Aluminium Company operated a narrow-gauge railway locally known as the 'puggie line' from their pier at the head of Loch Linnhe near the mouth of the River Lochy via Inverlochy to their Lochaber Works just north of the town. En route it crossed both the Mallaig and the Glasgow main railway lines. Seen here in 1955 is loco No. 1, *Sir Murray Morrison* (the engineer who played a very important role in the development of the Highland aluminium smelters and became the British Aluminium Company chief) heading a special train on the occasion of an enthusiasts' visit from the Light Railway Transport League. It was built in 1916 by Kerr, Stuart of Stoke on Trent for Balfour, Beatty & Co., the BA works' site contractor, which initially operated it before it passed to the aluminium company at Kinlochleven until 1929 when it was transferred to Fort William. It continued to be worked there until its sale in 1970 to the Hampshire Narrow Gauge Railway Society for preservation. During the peak site construction period in the 1920s, as many as 60 assorted steam, battery and petrol-driven locos were used on the 23 miles of three foot (and in some sections two foot) gauge line to Loch Treig and also between the dams at Loch Treig and Loch Laggan. Some of the small petrol 'speeders' (also familiarly known as 'cockroaches') had been converted from model T Ford cars to run on rails, as had a Ford van which became a railed ambulance. The last sections of the line progressively closed in the 1970s with total closure in 1977.

Left: The British Aluminium Company also ran an electric railway between their Kinlochleven smelter and the pier at the head of Loch Leven conveying raw materials inwards and the finished product outwards. Locos numbered 1 and 2 (one of which is seen here) were purchased for the inception of the line in 1908, while No. 3 arrived in 1947. All were four-wheelers built by Metropolitan–Vickers of Trafford Park, Manchester, and remained until 1960 when the line closed. The BA company merged with the Canadian Alcan company in the 1980s, but sadly their Kinlochleven complex shut down completely in 2000, bringing an end to over 90 years of mixed prosperity for the little town which waxed and waned along with the fortunes of the aluminium company.

One of the first cars in the Fort William area was a Paisley-built Arrol–Johnston owned by Alex (Sandy) and John MacPherson, who used it for hiring purposes. The MacPherson brothers, natives of Arisaig, were pioneers of motor transport in Lochaber, and Sandy had previously driven MacGregor & Cameron's horse-drawn mail coach between Fort William and Arisaig. Hardly surprisingly, when the West Highland Railway opened to Mallaig in 1901, the horse-drawn coaches admitted defeat and were withdrawn from the route. They were then employed instead on tourist drives to local attractions such as Glen Nevis, Glenfinnan, Glen Roy, Achnacarry and Loch Arkaig. The photograph on the left shows MacPherson's garage in Gordon Square, which was originally the stables of MacGregor & Cameron and had been home to a stud of 40 horses. The car, used for hiring purposes, is ST 1358, an 18 h.p. Rover landaulette of 1919.

A. & J. MacPherson went on to operate charabancs and buses in addition to their fleet of taxis and hire cars. Seen in Gordon Square are two charabancs advertising tours to Glen Nevis and to Kinlochleven and Glencoe. On the left is ST 4068, a Chevrolet fourteen-seater new in 1926 while ST 3177 was a 1925 Albion Viking with nineteen-seat bodywork by Cowieson of Glasgow (displaying a lucky lizard radiator mascot). In addition to the coach tours, bus services were operated to Corpach and to Glenfinnan. The business was sold to David MacBrayne in 1939.

MacPherson's Lochaber Motor Co. occupied the Parade Garage at the east end of Fort William from the late 1920s. It was run by Joe, son of previously mentioned Alex McPherson until the 1960s when demolition took place due to major redevelopment with the construction of the new dual-carriageway along the shore. This line-up of new Chevrolet light trucks and vans, plus assorted cars including Morris Cowley, Austin and Chevrolet, was photographed on a dull day in 1929. The Chev delivery van on the extreme left (ST 5657) at Lachlan Wynne's meat mart is lettered in the livery of Angus MacSwan, general merchants, of the Caledonian Warehouse, Corpach. Third Chev from left (ST 5611) was a 30 cwt. truck delivered to local haulage contractor Robert Heiton Drummond of Lochy Bridge who ran a carrier's service between Fort William and Glasgow. He sold his business to David MacBrayne in 1939. The two cars on the extreme right (ST 5617 & 5632) were owned respectively by Nigel MacKenzie of Caberfeidh, Fort William and John MacKintosh of Corpach Hotel. Also visible in this picture is the sign denoting the old London & North Eastern Railway goods station, another casualty of the new road.

The main motor garage in Fort William primarily catering for private customers was run by Marshall & Pearson in the High Street, whereas rivals in the town for commercial business were A. & J. MacPherson and A. MacIntyre & Sons. Archibald MacIntyre settled in Fort William in the late nineteenth century and set up an emporium and jewellers business in the High Street. A garage soon followed, with a Ford dealership later. Charabanc tours were operated from the early 1920s, then during the general strike of 1926 MacIntyre's provided a temporary bus service between Fort William and Glasgow. Also that year a regular daily run was started in July linking Fort William with Inverness, which was known as 'MacIntyre's Pioneer Service' as may be seen on the side panels of this Lancia 26-seater (GD 4771) which was new in 1926 and one of two purchased second-hand from Rankin Bros. of Glasgow. (Strictly speaking this was not a pioneer venture, since MacBraynes had run between the two towns prior to World War I and MacRae & Dick linked both ends of the Great Glen from June 1926.) The photo was taken not in service but at Tomonie, on the old road between Banavie and Corpach, with the great bulk of Ben Nevis just discernible. Note also that both front tyres are completely bald – not uncommon in the days long before legislation on tyre treads.

Problems arose on MacIntyre's Fort William to Inverness service with the various weak wooden bridges encountered in some of the places where the route crossed the Caledonian Canal; Tomnahurich Bridge just outside Inverness was particularly vulnerable to large vehicles, with the passengers having to disembark and walk across. Another problem was the weight limit at Oich Bridge, Aberchalder, which caused Archibald MacIntyre to be charged in May 1927 with crossing it in a 'car', the registered axle weight of which exceeded three tons on one axle, in breach of notices posted on the bridge. As a result, 26-seat buses like the Lancia were regarded as too heavy for the route and were replaced by several fourteen and twenty seat Fords. Three of these like ST 6276, illustrated right, were particularly interesting in that they were tri-axle six wheelers, designed to solve the axle weight restrictions, with chassis extensions by the Truck & Tractor Appliance Co. of Manchester and twenty-seat bodywork by J. H. Jennings of Sandbach, Cheshire, a company better known for building goods vehicle bodies. Being Ford agents, MacIntyres naturally focussed on Ford for their own fleet but also operated an assortment of AEC, Albion, Chevrolet, Fiat, Guy, Lancia and Overland buses.

This scene, between Invermoriston and Drumnadrochit is admittedly outwith Lochaber, but shows ST 6535, one of several fourteen-seater Fords new in 1931 which operated MacIntyre's mail service between Fort William and Inverness since a restriction had been placed on the canal bridge at Fort Augustus limiting buses to a maximum of fourteen seats. The year of this scene is 1934 when final construction work was being carried out during the improvements to the Great Glen road along the north side of Loch Ness, which became known as the Glen Albyn Highway when officially opened in September of that year. The ceremony was performed by Leslie Hore-Belisha, the serving Minister of Transport, who was responsible for the introduction of pedestrian crossings and also driving tests.

In addition to the Ford dealership and bus services, MacIntyre's also operated a haulage contracting and car hire business. In 1930, at his Monzie Square premises on the corner of Fort William High Street (now Edinburgh Woollen Mill) we see Archie MacIntyre on the left along with ST 5985, a Ford model AA six-wheel lorry and ST 6116, a model A Ford 'Fordor' saloon car, both new that year. To the rear are the Lochaber Dairy and Springbank Temperance Hotel. Advertisements in the window of MacIntyre's garage offer the Ford Fordor (four door) at £225 and the 'Tudor' (two door) at £195, while another notice gives the opportunity to 'test the safe, dependable new Ford in a reliability run of your own'. MacIntyre had another garage in town for the buses and lorries adjacent to his west end home at Fassifern Villa.

A photograph taken in the mid-1930s in the High Street at Monzie Square opposite the Palace Hotel. Archie MacIntyre is seen leaning against YT 2665 (a Minerva hire car new the previous decade) whilst in deep discussion with a group of local ladies, no doubt about the dilemma of different destinations for a journey by car or in one of his buses. A sign on the corner advertises the Fort William to Inverness bus service, which was shared with MacRae & Dick of Inverness and Fort William and offered several daily departures. MacIntyre's original timetable for 1926 (reproduced here) allowed four hours for a journey which is covered today in one hour fifty minutes by Scottish Citylink coaches. By 1934 the journey time had been cut to three hours, reflecting the road improvements through the Great Glen. In 1936 A. MacIntyre & Sons sold their bus services to MacBraynes who were slowly but surely extending their sphere of operations in the area, at which point Archie MacIntyre became their motor services inspector in Fort William.

Angus Warren of Ballachulish was a coachman on the horse-drawn coaches to Glencoe and then operated his own motor charabancs and buses in the 1920s, by which time of course the motor vehicle had taken a major foothold. Warren's Lancia charabanc ES 8508 (note the separate door to each row of seats), awaits a private group at Ballachulish Ferry station in the summer of 1934 from the Oban train, which judging by the puffs of steam has arrived. This charabanc was new in 1926 to Peter Crerar of Crieff who had a large fleet of these fast Italian chassis which usually received bodywork built at Crerar's own coachworks. Ballachulish Ferry was the last station before the terminus at Ballachulish on the railway line from Oban, a casualty of Dr Beeching's axe in 1966. It had opened as a branch from Connel Ferry on the Callander & Oban Railway in 1903 and was therefore one of the last lines built in Britain. The old platform may still be seen today amongst the undergrowth behind Ballachulish Hotel.

SB 3866 was a Chevrolet fourteen-seater bought new by Angus Warren in 1931 to operate not only the Glencoe tour from Kentallen pier but also a joint service between Ballachulish station and Tyndrum station which was shared with MacConnacher of Ballachulish. Trouble in the Glen, perhaps, as two heads are bent over the bonnet attempting to solve the engine problem. The scene is near Kingshouse looking towards Glencoe, guarded by Buachaille Etive Mor, the mountain known as 'the great shepherd of Etive'. Hardly the place to stop in the middle of the road on today's busy A82, but traffic was still sparse in the 1930s. Warren's business was acquired in 1936 by David MacBrayne, along with one Commer bus.

OEH 461 was a second-hand Guy Vixen of 1950 owned by MacConnacher with coachwork built by Ormac of Preston and seen here in 1963 in Ballachulish village. In the mid-1980s, Alex MacConnacher of Brecklet Garage introduced his successful 'Gaelic Bus' fleet to the Lochaber area in opposition to Highland Buses. Coast-to-coast connecting services were operated from Oban in the west to Inverness in the east and town services in Fort William, but in 1995 the business was sold.

The Glencoe and Glenetive tour mentioned on page 4 continued to operate from horse days (apart from suspension during the 1939–45 wartime years) until the closure of the Oban to Ballachulish branch railway line in 1966. Until this time, passengers would leave Oban by the 9.42 a.m. train for Ballachulish (arriving at 11.14) where Alexander MacConnacher provided a connecting motor coach which departed at 11.20. After a refreshment break at Glencoe Hotel – also owned by MacConnacher – the coach motored via the 'Glen of Weeping' and turned off the main highway onto the narrow road through the ancient Royal Deer Forest of Dalness and into Glen Etive. At 1.45 from Lochetivehead the tourists would sail on the well-appointed yacht *Darthula II* which included dining facilities and was a far cry from the old *Ossian* of earlier years. Arriving at Achnacloich at 3.45 p.m. there was comfortable time to join the 4.09 p.m. Oban train to complete the circle. Alternatively the tour could be taken in the opposite direction, setting off from Oban by the 9.30 a.m. Glasgow train as far as Achnacloich. This view, taken in Glen Etive in 1937, shows SB 5348 which was one of two similar Guy Wolf fourteen-seaters bodied by James Martin of Kirkintilloch and purchased that year by MacConnacher. This bus lives on, as it escaped the usual fate of time-expired vehicles and was saved for restoration, being preserved in England.

This early scene on Fort William pier shows three of the five 20 h.p. Commer fifteen-seater charabancs purchased in 1911 by David MacBrayne, and which carried names rather than numbers (*Hare, Hound, Stag, Weasel* and *Wolf*). These vehicles were supplied by the Lanarkshire Motor Company, Scottish agents for Commer cars, hence the registration numbers V 1561/2, and were used partly to work a new service between Fort William and Inverness. The logic here was possibly because of the cessation in 1911 of the Invergarry & Fort Augustus Railway operations, despite MacBraynes own paddle steamer *Gondolier* sailing the length of the Caledonian Canal from Banavie to Inverness. The only names known in this view are those of Mr A. Burgess, MacBraynes local agent around the end of World War I and drivers Fraser to the left and K. MacKenzie centre.

At the same location about 1950 we see MacBraynes Commer buses again. Although a giant step ahead of the primitive charabancs in the previous view, a coach driver of today would nevertheless regard these late 1940s vehicles as positively vintage. On the left is No. 16 (GGG 188) leaving for Ballachulish and to the right 71 (FGG 636). Both were Commer Commandos bodied by Croft of Gallowgate, Glasgow. Also visible is L111 (FUS 542) a Thornycroft Nippy mail van and one of the Maudslay Marathon coaches of the same period.

A 1937 view of Fort William bus station and the hills of Ardgour beyond Loch Linnhe. Surprisingly perhaps, MacBraynes operated few Albions in their fleet. Apart from one or two very early models in 1907 when the bus fleet was still in its infancy, only five new Albion buses were ever purchased. One of these (bound for North Ballachulish) is seen in the centre of this trio. It was No. 56 (US 2008), which was one of three delivered in 1933 with twenty-seat Park Royal bodywork incorporating a mail compartment. The Albion on the left was inherited with the acquisition of Major J. H. Shields' Kinlochleven Motor Company in 1934. This was No. 62 (GG 9318), a Cowieson-bodied 26-seater which had been new in 1932 and had originally operated for Carmichael of Glenboig. The Bedford coach for Inverness was 84 (YS 8468), a twenty-seat Duple-bodied WTB model which was one of seven delivered in 1936. One of the earlier Maudslays in the fleet is just visible beyond.

Paddle wheels pounding, MacBraynes venerable vessel *Iona* churns the waters of Loch Linnhe as she steams from Fort William to Oban through the Corran Narrows past Ardgour pier and Corran lighthouse. On certain days and by arrangement, the Oban steamer would call at Ardgour, Onich, Kentallen and the Isle of Lismore but by the 1935 season the timetable had dropped Ardgour and Onich although made an additional conditional call at Appin pier. This scene looks towards Ben Keil from Nether Lochaber and dates from 1935, which was the final season of service for the one-time flagship of the fleet. *Iona* was the third ship so-named and was built in 1864 at J. & G. Thomson's Govan yard on the Clyde for the Hutcheson brothers – predecessors of their later partner David MacBrayne who assumed full control in 1879. After an incredible 72 years in Clyde and West Highland waters, *Iona* was broken up by Arnott, Young & Co. at Dalmuir. The first regular sailings connecting Glasgow with Oban and Fort William had been made by Henry Bell's pioneering steamship *Comet* of 1812, which met her fate when wrecked in Loch Craignish in 1820.

Apart from the various local service bus runs operated by MacBraynes from their base in Fort William, a number of day and half-day excursions, some of which included a steamer sailing, were offered to tourists during the summer season (the front cover illustrates a classic example). One of the full-day excursions from the town was to the Ardnamurchan peninsula, which involved crossing Loch Linnhe by the Corran Ferry then driving by Loch Sunart to the lighthouse at Ardnamurchan Point. This scene from the mid-1960s shows No. 183 (607 CYS), one of MacBraynes Duple-bodied 29-seat Bedford coaches leaving the council-operated ferry at Ardgour which at that time charged ten shillings for the bus plus fourpence per passenger for the single crossing. The 1959 Bedford lorry (USF 223) on the ferry was owned by Arnott McLeod of Edinburgh, a firm of building and civil engineering contractors which carried out much construction work in the West Highlands. Driving the tour coach on this occasion was Angus (Plum) Cameron of Fort William. Other drivers at Fort William depot included Jimmy Gordon, Jimmy MacLean, Hugh (Pongo) Cameron, Ian MacLaren, Angus MacIntyre and Alistair Sinclair to name but a few.

Looking down Fort William's Station Brae in the late 1940s, when the railway station still carried its LNER name sign above the entrance. Leaving its stance at the bus depot on the local service to Inverlochy is one of three wartime utility Bedford OWB models with Duple bodywork delivered to MacBraynes in 1943. This was No. 24 (DUS 24). The lorry with its nose towards Loch Linnhe was also a wartime Bedford – the square-nosed OY type which was one of the large fleet in service with the Royal Navy – while just visible to the left is the cab of MacBrayne No. 64 (EGA 641), a 1947 Park Royal bodied AEC Regal.

With school over for the day and housewives heading home after shopping, MacBraynes afternoon bus at 4.10 from Fort William to Onich, North Ballachulish and Kinlochleven was a busy departure. No. 30 (KGG 710), one of three Roe bodied AEC Regal half-cabs of 1953, is seen at the bus station in the early 1960s with the railway station entrance beyond. MacBraynes local managers successively lived in the apartment above the office in this 1930s art deco style building (similar to MacBrayne pier offices at other locations) until it was demolished in the 1970s to make way for the new dual carriageway along the shore. The bus station was then relocated next to the new railway station at the east end of the town. This 4.10 p.m. journey was worked by MacBraynes Kinlochleven depot, where two of the drivers included brothers John and Willie Gray, with depot controller Donald Robertson in charge. Kinlochleven Depot was acquired in 1934 with the business of John H. Shields who later held a senior position with MacBraynes.

As its transport hub, the station square was always an area of bustling activity in Fort William, with bus and railway stations adjacent to the nearby pier. This scene from summer 1963 shows the MacBrayne steamer *Lochnevis* on the Fort William to Oban service and an assortment of MacBraynes road vehicles. No. 178 (UGB 428), the first of many AEC Reliance 41-seat coaches delivered from 1958 until 1962 with Duple Midland Donington style bodies is right foreground, while on the left is 86 (384 FGB) a Bedford VAS service bus with 21-seat Duple Midland bodywork new in 1962. The other Bedford is 69 (373 FGB) a 1962 Duple-bodied Bella Vista 29-seat coach and GGA 575, the elderly lorry, is L120 of 1948, a seven ton Maudslay Mogul in its fifteenth and final year of service with MacBrayne.

Timber! Bus driver Angus Maclean assesses the problem after one of the planks on Fort William pier has given way under the weight of MacBraynes Albion lorry L2, captured on camera in 1960. This vehicle had an interesting pedigree, having started life as a twenty-seater bus with Skye Transport in 1949. MacBraynes acquired this Scottish Co-operative Wholesale Society-owned company in 1958 and converted GGA 989 to a lorry the following year. Also in view are bus 23 (WGG 623) a 28-seat Duple (Midland) bodied Bedford of 1959 and 35 (FGB 418) a Maudslay of 1947 rebodied in 1958 by Duple. **37**

MacBraynes inherited their bus routes on the Ardnamurchan peninsula when Ardgour & Acharacle Motor Services Ltd. of Acharacle was acquired in 1951, but did not retain any of that company's vehicles. Services operated were from the Corran Ferry at Ardgour to Strontian, Salen and Acharacle with a connection to Glenborrodale, Kilmory and Kilchoan (the most westerly point on the British mainland served by bus). Driver Hugh Livingstone of Kilchoan had previously worked with the A&AMS and before that with James Allan of Glenborrodale who had been the original operator between Kilchoan and Acharacle in 1927. Hugh is seen here in 1960 at the wheel of MacBraynes Bedford OLAZ No. 160 (KGD 901), one of 22 similar buses delivered in 1952 mainly for remote rural routes. Its Duple Sportsman body had only thirteen seats but a large luggage and mail compartment which was necessary to carry the wide variety of goods, parcels and deliveries of bread and cakes to the village store at Kilchoan and farms and crofts along the route. Every morning except Sundays, Hugh would set off on the 7 a.m. departure for Acharacle, to wind his way along the shores of Loch Sunart. Parcels and mails (and occasionally even passengers) would be transferred at Salen for Ardgour and the Corran Ferry and onward connections to Fort William.

MacBraynes 7 a.m. bus from Kilchoan to Acharacle connected en route at Salen, Loch Sunart with the 8.30 a.m. from Acharacle to Ardgour, which in turn connected with the Corran Ferry for the Nether Lochaber shore. Here we see the turntable ferry arriving from Ardgour for the connection onwards to Fort William which was the 10 a.m. service from Kinlochleven, North Ballachulish and Onich. MacBraynes No. 35 has been reversed down to the ferry by Hugh (Pongo) Cameron of Onich who delighted in driving almost to the water's edge on the seaweed covered slipway, often to the concern of his passengers. After loading the mail and passengers from Ardnamurchan the journey was scheduled to continue

from Corran Ferry at 10.35 a.m., for arrival in Fort William at 11 a.m. The bus seen here had an interesting although perhaps confusing pedigree. Delivered in 1947, No. 35 (FGB 418) was a half-cab Maudslay Marathon originally with a second-hand Park Royal body of 1936 which had been a replacement initially fitted to 29 (SB 3362), a 1929 Maudslay Meteor which started life with Hall Lewis coachwork. The Duple bodywork in this 1960 scene had been built in 1958, and the bus was withdrawn by MacBraynes in 1967 but enjoyed further service with Garner's buses, Bridge of Weir.

Representative of MacBraynes road transport fleet in the 1950s and 60s in the Lochaber area was lorry No. L9 (BST 176), an Austin K2. This vehicle had started life in 1946 as a nineteen-seat bus with McKinnon of Lochboisdale, South Uist, and after that firm sold out to MacBrayne in 1947 it continued as their bus No. 82 until conversion to a lorry in 1957. As it passes Ballachulish Hotel in summer 1962, part of the lengthy queue of cars waiting to cross the ferry can be seen; a queue which continued to lengthen each year until 1975 when Ballachulish Bridge opened.

MacBraynes lorry L127 (814 KGB) was a Bedford TK model new in 1963 and pulled an articulated unit. It is seen here on the main Fort William to Inverness road near Laggan locks at the northern end of Loch Lochy. L127 and others in the road transport fleet operated regularly from the Scottish Wool Growers factory in Paisley to Kyle of Lochalsh where their loads of woollen bales were transferred to MacBraynes MV *Loch Seaforth* for the crossing of the Minch to Stornoway in Lewis.

A feature of many of MacBraynes rural bus services was the collection and delivery of mails along the route. Often the buses were fitted with mail boxes and could be hailed simply to post a letter. On other routes the driver or conductor emptied the roadside mail boxes, as instanced on the service between North Ballachulish and Fort William. Driver Angus MacLean of Claggan was a Skyeman who worked from MacBraynes Fort William depot. This scene from the early 1960s shows him unlocking a mailbox at Onich on a morning run into the Fort from North Ballachulish. His coach was 1961 Duple-bodied 29-seat Bedford No. 181 (605 CYS).

This 1964 view shows conductress Valerie MacLeod (now MacDonald) of Fort William on the same service as that on the facing page emptying the mailbox at Springbank, Onich. The bus on this journey was 191 (AYS 737B), a Bedford VAS with 28-seat Duple (Midland) service bus bodywork. Today of course the post office is totally responsible for these collections and the days when the bus crews doubled as postmen and women are but a distant memory. Inset on this view is a MacBrayne card ticket of the type issued prior to the introduction of paper roll tickets used in the Setright machine worn by Valerie.

43

Lochy Bridge at Mallaig road end, where the A830 meets the main A82 to Inverness, as it appeared in the late 1950s. The scene is now much altered and is controlled by traffic lights, while the old bridge and its archways at either side of the River Lochy have been demolished to make way for today's wider but less attractive replacement. MacBraynes bus heading into town from Corpach is No. 37 (KGG 712), one of two 44-seat AEC Regal IVs with bodywork by Charles Roe of Leeds. These 1953 deliveries were the first underfloor engined buses in the fleet.

Summer Sunday at Altnafeadh, 1964. The crew of the northbound MacBrayne coach for Fort William have just swapped over with their counterparts on the southbound Glasgow service. On weekdays this took place at Kinlochleven but on Sundays the morning departure from Glasgow was 1 hour 15 minutes later, thus requiring the different changeover point. On Mondays to Saturdays this summer-only service continued to Inverness via the Great Glen, but terminated at Fort William on Sundays. The vehicles in this view are No. 12 on the left and No. 47 right. The former (KGG 708) was an AEC Regal new in 1953 with Roe bodywork of the half-cab style seen on page 34, which had been rebodied in 1961 with new Duple full-fronted coachwork to give a more modern appearance. No. 47 (WGG 636) was an AEC Reliance of 1959 with Duple (Midland) coachwork which survived to see further service with Highland Omnibuses when MacBraynes operations passed to the Scottish Transport Group in 1970, thus bringing 65 years of MacBrayne buses to an end.

A frosting of snow covers the bulk of Ben Nevis in the background of this wintry scene in December 1964 as MacBraynes AEC Reliance No. 198 (CGA 568B) crosses the old canal bridge at Banavie. This bus was only a few months old at the time and was one of the two largest in the fleet. Delivered in the summer of 1964, 197 and 198 had 53-seat Willowbrook bodies and were normally used on the busy local route between Fort William and Corpach, serving the employees at the then new pulp mill. The earliest bus operator on this service in the 1920s and 30s was the partnership of Peter Cruickshank and Ernest Clark of Viewfield Lane, Fort William with a mixed fleet of Chevrolet, Pierce Arrow, Spa and Studebaker fourteen-seaters.

The section of the A82 road between Glencoe and Kinlochleven was still commonly referred to as the 'German Road' when I drove MacBraynes buses over it in the 1960s. (German prisoners of the 1914–18 war interned at Kinlochleven had carried out most of its construction.) Until Ballachulish Bridge opened in 1975, much of the traffic for Fort William and beyond took this route to avoid the bottleneck at the ferry crossing and so the road then carried heavier traffic than subsequently. This accident scene from the summer of 1964 shows a long line of traffic delayed during the recovery of an Army-owned Ford Thames with

Rootes Group cab which had nearly toppled to Loch Leven below. The rescuers were both six-cylinder Scammells; a Meadows petrol-engined example in the foreground accompanied by a Gardner diesel model, both probably sent to assist from Scottish Command REME workshops at Stirling. Both Scammells have the cycle type front wings which turned with the wheels. Visible in the traffic queue are two AEC Reliance coaches, the first operating MacBraynes Glasgow to Inverness service (which I had abandoned to take this photo). It was one of several with Duple Donington bodies and is followed by a Plaxton-bodied example on tour to the Isle of Skye with Wallace Arnold Tours. The cable incorporated in the safety fencing alongside the German Road had originally been used on the British Aluminium Company's site at Kinlochleven as part of the 'Blondin' or aerial steel ropeway strung on pylons which carried buckets of materials and supplies to the workings at Blackwater Dam.

A Victorian view at Corpach Hotel in the 1890s where at that time the proprietor was Colin McPherson. Passing towards Annat is a four-wheel cart with back-to-back seating drawn by a single horse and known as a dogcart phaeton. Outside the front door a two-horse wagonette awaits with two ladies and two gentlemen already on board. Seating in this type of carriage was for three passengers on each of the two inward-facing benches, while the coachman had an elevated seat with an angled footboard. Apart from minor alterations, the appearance of Corpach Hotel remains much the same today.